D1825153

Continual
Dew

By the same Author

MOUNT ZION
GHASTLY GOOD TASTE

All rights reserved

CONTINUAL DEW

A LITTLE BOOK
OF
BOURGEOIS VERSE

by

John Betjeman

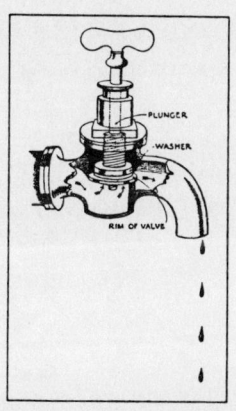

LONDON
JOHN MURRAY, ALBEMARLE STREET, W

First Edition, 1937
Facsimile reissue, 1977

Printed in Great Britain
Photo-litho reprint by W & J Mackay Limited, Chatham
From earlier impression
0 7195 3395 3

Contents

TO

GERALD BERNERS

The last fifteen poems in this book appeared in " Mount Zion " (James Press) and Mr. Edward James gave kind and ready permission to the author to reprint them.

The following artists supplied sympathetic illustrations. Mr. de Cronin Hastings (pp. 35, 36, 38, 40, 42) Mr. E. McKnight Kauffer (the dust jacket), Mr. Osbert Lancaster (the cover, pp. 14 and 15 and the decorative borders to the lines on Calvinistic Evensong), Mr. Gabriel Pippet (the art nouveau decoration to Exeter). Other pictures are from various pre-war sources. Lord Longford corrected the proofs and did the orthography, never a strong point of the author's, though he is indebted to Mr. C. S. Lewis for the fact on page 256.

He also wishes to thank the editors of the NEW OXFORD OUTLOOK, MOTLEY (Dublin Gate Theatre), THE LONDON MERCURY and OXFORD AND CAMBRIDGE for permission to reprint some of these verses.

THE ARREST OF OSCAR WILDE AT THE
CADOGAN HOTEL

E sipped at a weak hock and seltzer
   As he gazed at the London skies
Through the Nottingham lace of the curtains
   Or was it his bees-winged eyes ?

To the right and before him Pont Street
   Did tower in her new built red,
As hard as the morning gaslight
   That shone on his unmade bed.

" I want some more hock in my seltzer,
   And Robbie, please give me your hand—
Is this the end or beginning ?
   How can I understand ?

" So you've brought me the latest *Yellow Book* :
   And Buchan has got in it now :
Approval of what is approved of
   Is as false as a well-kept vow.

" More hock, Robbie—where is the seltzer ?
   Dear boy, pull again at the bell !
They are all little better than *cretins*,
   Though this *is* the Cadogan Hotel.

" One astrakhan coat is at Willis's—
   Another one's at the Savoy :
Do fetch my morocco portmanteau,
   And bring them on later, dear boy."

I

A thump, and a murmur of voices—
    (" Oh why must they make such a din ? ")
As the door of the bedroom swung open
    And TWO PLAIN CLOTHES POLICEMEN came in :

" Mr Woilde, we 'ave come for tew take yew
    Where felons and criminals dwell :
We must ask yew tew leave with us quoietly
    For this *is* the Cadogan Hotel."

He rose, and he put down *The Yellow Book*.
    He staggered—and, terrible-eyed,
He brushed past the palms on the staircase
    And was helped to a hansom outside.

DISTANT VIEW OF A PROVINCIAL TOWN

ESIDE those spires so spick and span
 Against an unencumbered sky
The old Great Western Railway ran
 When someone different was I.

St Aidan's with the prickly nobs
 And iron spikes and coloured tiles—
Where Auntie Maud devoutly bobs
 In those enriched vermilion aisles.

St George's where the mattins bell
 But rarely drowned the trams for prayer—
No Popish sight or sound or smell
 Disturbed that gas-invaded air.

St Mary's where the Rector preached
 In such a jolly friendly way
On cricket, football, things that reached
 The simple life of every day.

And that United Benefice
 With entrance permanently locked,—
How Gothic, grey and sad it is
 Since Mr Grogley was unfrocked!

The old Great Western Railway shakes,
 The old Great Western Railway spins—
The old Great Western Railway makes
 Me very sorry for my sins.

SLOUGH

OME, friendly bombs, and fall on Slough !
It isn't fit for humans now ,
There isn't grass to graze a cow.
Swarm over, Death !

Come, bombs, and blow to smithereens
Those air-conditioned, bright canteens,
Tinned fruit, tinned meat, tinned milk, tinned beans,
Tinned minds, tinned breath.

Mess up the mess they call a town—
A house for ninety-seven down
And once a week a half a crown
For twenty years.

And get that man with double chin
Who'll always cheat and always win,
Who washes his repulsive skin
In women's tears :

And smash his desk of polished oak
And smash his hands so used to stroke
And stop his boring dirty joke
And make him yell.

But spare the bald young clerks who add
The profits of the stinking cad ;
It's not their fault that they are mad,
They've tasted Hell.

4

It's not their fault they do not know
The birdsong from the radio,
It's not their fault they often go
        To Maidenhead

And talk of sport and makes of cars
In various bogus-Tudor bars
And daren't look up and see the stars
        But belch instead.

In labour-saving homes, with care
Their wives frizz out peroxide hair
And dry it in synthetic air
        And paint their nails.

Come, friendly bombs and fall on Slough
To get it ready for the plough.
The cabbages are coming now ;
        The earth exhales.

PUBLIC HOUSE DRUNK

Bass Turn again, Higginson,
Treble   *thrice Mayor of London!*
Bass Stretch the bow of your bells,
Treble   *Saint Mary's steeple!*
Bass Finsbury, Highbury,
Treble   *you are all undone!*
Bass Moorfields and Cripplegate,
Treble   *wake up your people!*

Bass	Saint Andrew Undershaft,
Treble	*Saint Andrew Hubbard,*
Bass	Saint Catherine Coleman,
Treble	*Saint Botolph, Saint Brides'*
Bass	Where are your registers ?
Treble	*in vestry cupboard*
Bass	Look him up, Higginson,
Treble	*find where he hides !*

Bass	Out of the Jew's Harp House,
Treble	*Old Mother Redcap*
Bass	Turn down the gas again
Treble	*—gas again, Glory !*
Bass	Clean up the bar in the
Treble	*wake of that madcap*
Bass	Lord Mayor of London ! Oh
Treble	*Lord what a story !*

Bass	Hold him down, Higginson !
Treble	*send for the beadles !*
Bass	" Fourteen, Macaulay street
Treble	*Bromley-by-Bow*
Bass	Represents pen-nibs
Treble	*steel holders and needles*
Bass	For the Office Equipment
Treble	*Efficiency Co."*

7

SUICIDE ON JUNCTION ROAD STATION AFTER ABSTENTION FROM EVENING COMMUNION IN NORTH LONDON

ITH the roar of the gas my heart gives a shout—
To Jehovah Tsidkenu the praise !
Bracket and bracket go blazen it out
In this Evangelical haze !

Jehovah Jireh ! the arches ring,
   The Mintons glisten, and grand
Are the surpliced boys as they sweetly sing
   On the threshold of glory land.

Jehovah Nisi ! from Tufnell Park,
   Five minutes to Junction Road,
Through grey brick Gothic and London dark,
   And my sins, a fearful load.

Six on the upside ! six on the down side !
   One gaslight in the Booking Hall
And a thousand sins on this lonely station,—
   What shall I do with them all ?

HEN the great bell
BOOMS
Over the Portland
stone urn,
And from the carved cedar wood
Rises the odour of incense,
I SIT DOWN
In St Botolph Bishops-
gate Churchyard,
And wait for the spirit of
my grandfather
Toddling along from the
Barbican.

CLASH went the Billiard balls in the Clerkenwell Social
Saloon.
Shut up the shutters and turn down the gas they'll
be calling the coppers in soon.
Goodnight, Alf !
Goodnight, Bert !
Goodnight, Mrs Gilligan !
Rain in the archway, no trams in the street.
COP COP
Cop on the cobbleway
Quick little ladylike feet
" 'Ard luck, aint got a gentleman ? "
" Not on a night like this, sweet "
" The Red Lion, Myddleton, all the 'ole lot of 'em
Shut but a light in The Star
Counting the coppers to see what they've got of 'em
Glistening wet in the bar
32, 34, 36, 38, Gaskin's not back with 'is tart
Left the 'all door open gives 'imself airs 'e does
Thinks 'imself too bloody smart
Gas on in the 'all and it's we've got to pay for it
Damn these old stairs and this bug-ridden panelling
See 'im tomorrow what 'e's got to say for it
Get on the bed there and start."

LOVE IN A VALLEY

AKE me, Lieutenant, to that Surrey homestead!
Red comes the winter and your rakish car,
Red among the hawthorns, redder than the hawberries
Or trails of old man's nuisance, and noisier far.
Far, far below me roll the Coulsdon woodlands,
White down the valley curves the living rail,*
Tall, tall, above me, olive spike the pinewoods,
Olive against blue black, moving in the gale.

Deep down the drive go the cushioned rhododendrons,
Deep down, sand deep, drives the heather root,
Deep the spliced timber barked around the summer house,
Light lies the tennis court, plantain underfoot.
What a winter welcome to what a Surrey homestead!
Oh! the metal lantern and white enamelled door!
Oh! the spread of orange from the gas fire on the carpet!
Oh! the tiny patter, sandalled footsteps on the floor!

Fling wide the curtains!—there's a Surrey sunset!
Low down the line sings the Addiscombe train,
Leaded are the windows lozenging the crimson,
Drained dark the pines in resin-scented rain.
Portable Lieutenant! that they carry you to China
And me to lonely shopping in a brilliant arcade;
Firm hand, fond hand switch the giddy engine!
So for us a last time is bright light made.

* Southern Electric 25 mins.

ITHIN that parsonage
There is a personage
Who owns a mortgage
  On his Lordship's land,
On his fine plantations,
Well speculated,
With groves of beeches
  On either hand—
On his ten ton schooner
Upon Loch Gowna,
And the silver birches
  Along the land—
Where the little pebbles
Do sing like trebles
As the waters bubble
  Upon the strand—

On his gateway olden
Of plaster moulded
And his splendid carriage way
  To Castle Grand,
(They've been aquatinted
For a book that's printed
And even wanted
  In far England)
His fine saloons there
Would make you swoon, sir,
And each surrounded
  By a gilded band—

And 'tis there Lord Ashtown
Lord Trimlestown and
Clonmore's Lord likewise
   Are entertained.

As many flunkeys
As Finnea has donkeys
Are there at all times
   At himself's command.
Though he doesn't pay them
They all obey him
And would sure die for him
   If he waved his hand ;
Yet if His Lordship
Comes for to worship
At the Holy Table
   To take his stand,
Though humbly kneeling
There's no fair dealing
And no kind feeling
   In the parson's hand.

Preaching of Liberty
Also of Charity
In the grand high pulpit
   To see him stand,
You'ld think that personage
In that parsonage
Did own no mortgage
   On His Lordship's land.

13

OUR PADRE

OUR padre is an old sky pilot,
    Severely now they've clipped his wings,
But still the flagstaff in the Rect'ry garden
    Points to Higher Things.

Still he has got a hearty handshake ;
    Still he wears medals and a stole ;
His voice would reach to Heaven, *and* make
    The Rock of Ages Roll.

He's too sincere to join the high church,
    Worshipping idols for the Lord,
And, though the lowest church is my church,
    Our padre's Broad.

Our padre is an old sky pilot,
    He's tied a reef knot round my heart,
We'll be rock'd up to Heaven on a rare old tune—
    Come on—take part !

CHORUS
(*Sung*)
    Pull for the shore, sailor, pull for the shore !
    Heed not the raging billow, bend to the oar !

Bend to the oar before the padre !
    Proud, with the padre rowing stroke !
Good old padre !   God for the services !
    Row like smoke !

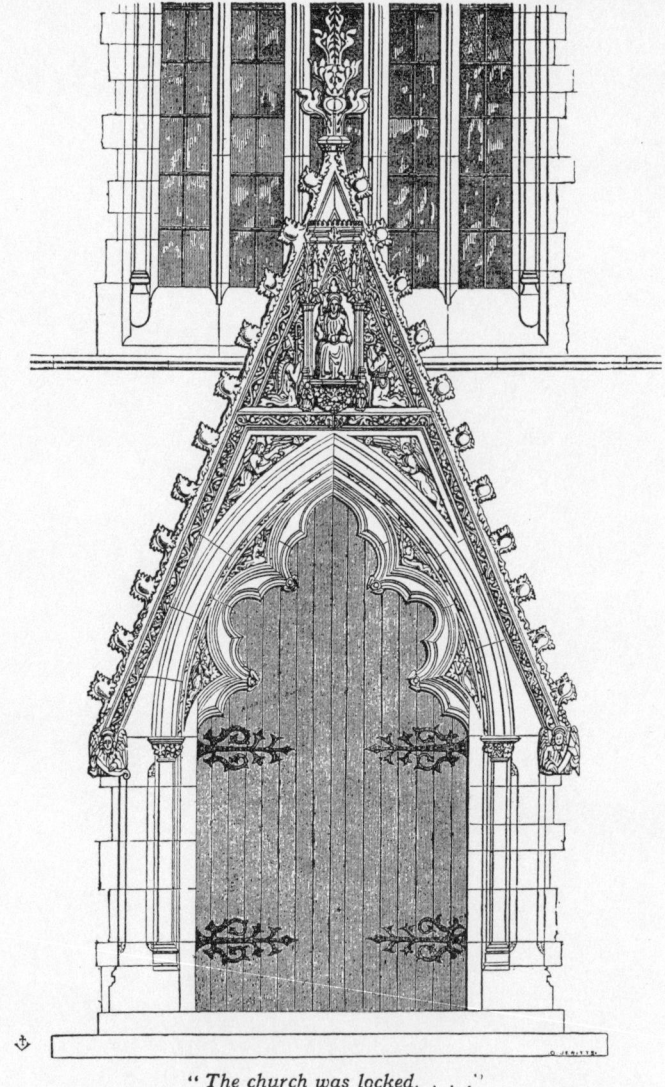

" The church was locked. . . ."

EXCHANGE OF LIVINGS

Lines suggested by an advertisement in "The Guardian"
(The Broad Church newspaper)

THE church was locked, so I went to the incumbent—
the incumbent enjoying a supine incumbency—
a tennis court, a summerhouse, deckchairs by the
walnut tree
and only the hum of the bees in the rockery.
" May I have the keys of the church, your incumbency ? "
" Yes, my dear sir, as a moderate churchman, I
am willing to exchange : light Sunday duty :
nice district : pop 149 : eight hundred per annum :
no extremes : A and M : bicyclist essential
same income expected."
" I think I'm the man that you want, your incumbency.
Here's my address when I'm not on my bicycle,
poking about for recumbent stone effigies—
14, Mount Ephraim, Cheltenham, Glos :
Rector St. George-in-the-Rolling Pins, Cripplegate :
non resident pop in the City of London :
eight fifty per annum (but verger an asset) :
willing to exchange (no extremes) for incumbency,
similar income, but closer to residence."

NDENOMINATIONAL
  But still the church of God
  He stood in his conventicle
  And ruled it with a rod.

Undenominational
  The walls around him rose
The lamps within their brackets shook
  To hear the hymns he chose.

" Glory " " Gopsal " " Russell Place "
  " Wrestling Jacob " " Rock "
" Saffron Walden " " Safe at Home "
  " Dorking " " Plymouth Dock "

I slipped about the chalky lane
  That runs without the park,
I saw the lone conventicle
  A beacon in the dark.

Revival ran along the hedge
  And made my spirit whole
When steam was on the window panes
  And glory in my soul.

DORSET

RIME Intrinsica, Fontmell Magna, Sturminster
Newton and Melbury Bubb
Whist upon whist upon whist upon whist drive, in
Institute, Legion and Social Club.
Horny hands that hold the aces which this morning
held the plough
While Tranter Reuben, T. S. Eliot, H. G. Wells and
Edith Sitwell lie in Mellstock Churchyard now.

Lord's Day bells from Bingham's Melcombe, Iwerne
Minster, Shroton, Plush,
Down the grass between the beeches, mellow in the
evening hush.

Gloved the hands that hold the hymn book, which
   this morning milked the cow
While Tranter Reuben, Mary Borden, Brian Howard
   and Harold Acton lie in Mellstock Churchyard
   now.

Light's abode, celestial Salem ! Lamps of evening,
   smelling strong,
Gleaming on the pitch pine waiting almost empty
   evensong ;
From the aisles each window smiles on grave and
   grass and yew tree bough,
While Tranter Reuben, Gordon Selfridge, Edna Best
   and Thomas Hardy lie in Mellstock Churchyard
   now.

> NOTE : *The names in the last lines of these
> stanzas are not put in out of malice or satire
> but merely for their euphony.*

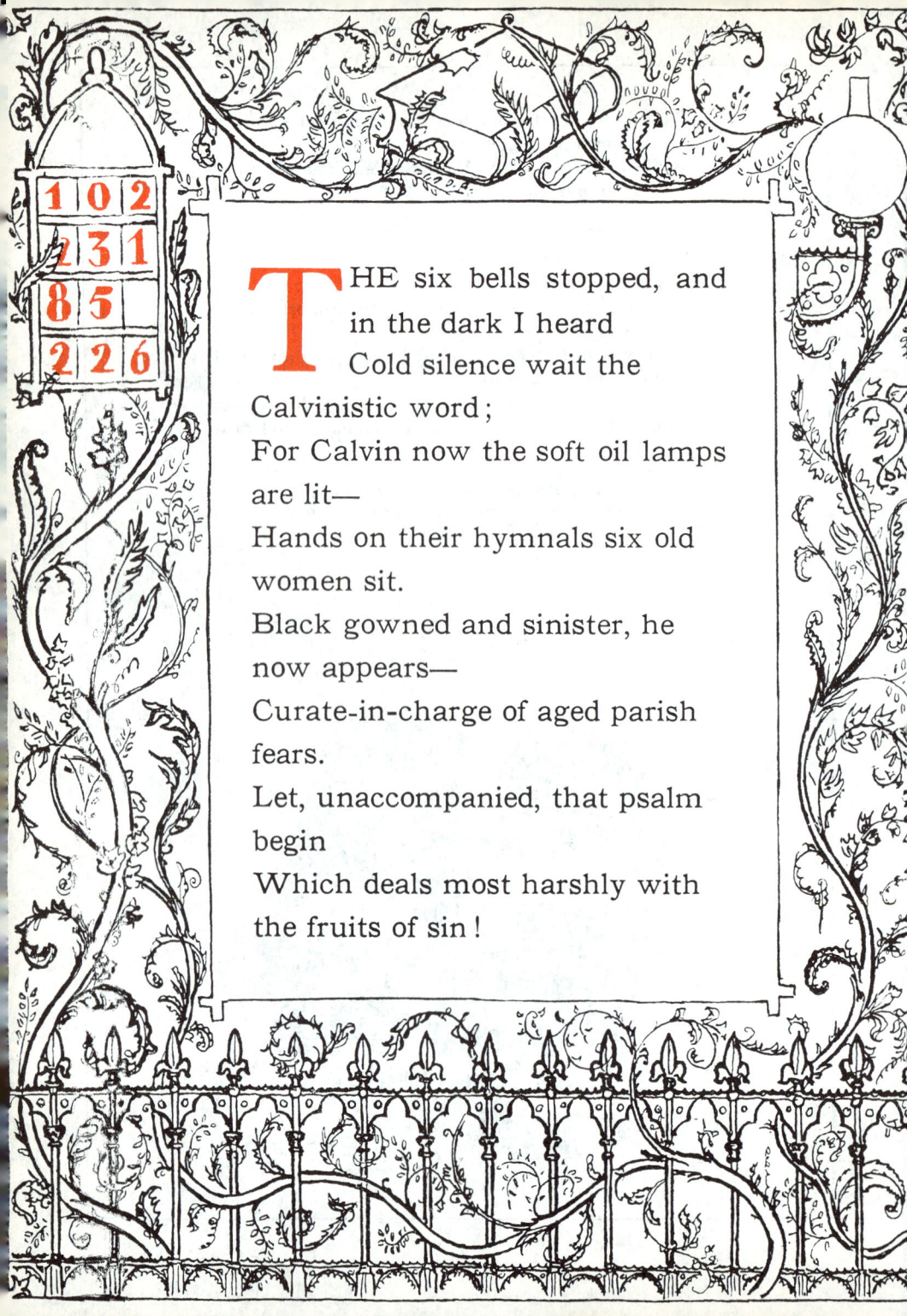

THE six bells stopped, and in the dark I heard
Cold silence wait the Calvinistic word;
For Calvin now the soft oil lamps are lit—
Hands on their hymnals six old women sit.
Black gowned and sinister, he now appears—
Curate-in-charge of aged parish fears.
Let, unaccompanied, that psalm begin
Which deals most harshly with the fruits of sin !

Boy! pump the organ! let the
anthem flow
With promise for the chosen
saints below!
Pregnant with warning the globed
elm trees wait—
Fresh coffin-wood beside the
churchyard gate.
And that mauve hat three
cherries decorate
Next week shall topple from its.
trembling perch
While wet fields reek like some
long empty church.

OSBERT LANCASTER

EXETER

The doctor's intellectual wife
Sat under the ilex tree
The Cathedral bells pealed over the wall
But never a bell heard she
And the sun played shadowgraphs on
her book
Which was writ by A. Huxléy.

Once those bells, those Exeter bells
Called her through Southernhaye
By pink, acacia-shaded walls
Several times a day
To Wilfric's altar and riddel posts
While the choir sang STANFORD in A

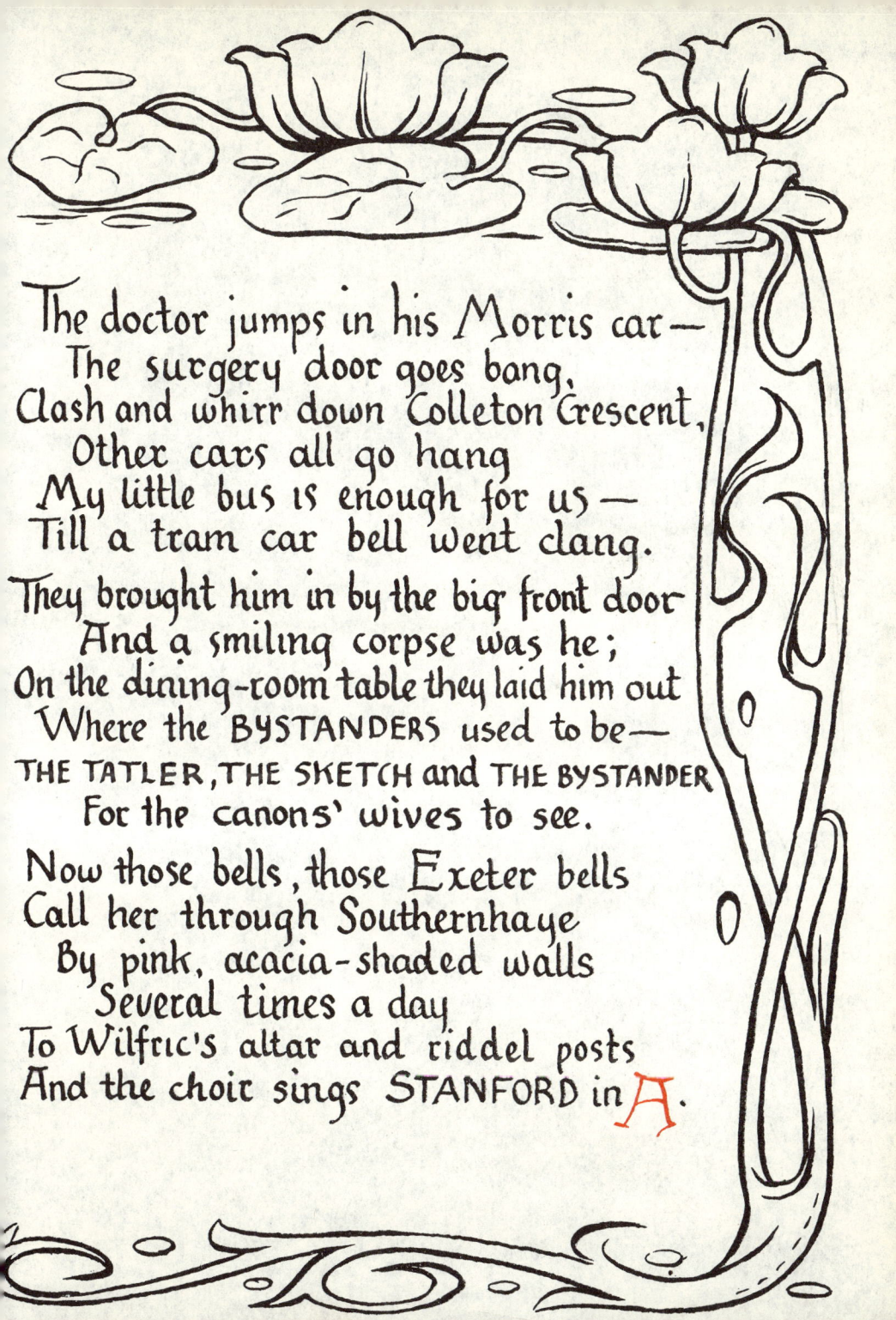

The doctor jumps in his Morris car—
 The surgery door goes bang,
Clash and whirr down Colleton Crescent,
 Other cars all go hang
 My little bus is enough for us—
 Till a tram car bell went clang.

They brought him in by the big front door
 And a smiling corpse was he;
On the dining-room table they laid him out
 Where the BYSTANDERS used to be—
THE TATLER, THE SKETCH and THE BYSTANDER
 For the canons' wives to see.

Now those bells, those Exeter bells
Call her through Southernhaye
 By pink, acacia-shaded walls
 Several times a day
To Wilfric's altar and riddel posts
And the choir sings STANFORD in A.

TEA WITH THE POETS

HREE pink Hampstead intellectuals,
Three thin *passé* Bloomsbury dons
Sit discussing Manley Hopkins
Over Mr. Grogley's dainty scones.

Three great hunks of bread and butter,
  Three great lumps of Cheddar cheese,
Big legs sprawling in the roadway
  Friends of Stephen Spender lie at ease.

Tucking in at whipped cream walnuts,
  Blue shorts bursting under green,
C. Day Lewis brings his wolf cubs
  Safe into the full canteen.

But when the Major lets the net down,
  When I see that cotton dress,
When we move to the verandah,
  When I put my racket in its press—

Then comes the tea time of all I like best
With my long-leggéd, blubber-lipped,
        carefree, uncorsetted,
          fun-freckled
        PRIMULA GUEST.

A HIKE ON THE DOWNS

" ES, rub some soap upon your feet !
    We'll hike round Winchester for weeks—
Like ancient Britons—just we two—
    Or more perhaps like ancient Greeks.

" You take your pipe—that will impress
    Your strength on anyone who passes ;
I'll take my *Plautus* (*non purgatus*)
    And both my pairs of horn-rimmed glasses.

" I've got my first, and now I know
    What life is and what life contains—
For, being just a first year man
    You don't meet all the first-class brains.

" Objectively, our Common Room
    Is like a small Athenian State—
Except for Lewis : he's all right
    But do you think he's *quite* first rate ?

" Hampshire mentality is low,
    And that is why they stare at us.
Yes, here's the earthwork—but it's dark ;
    We may as well return by bus."

THE WYKEHAMIST AT HOME

"KNOCK'D out my pipe on my old flannel bags,
    I lay back and thought about Kant.
Bees humm'd the solicitor's garden in ;
    I am empiric : bees aren't.

" I felt for my 'baccy jar up on a shelf
    With its New College Crest done in yellow.
Boys called in the Methodist Sunday School—
    I am a sociable fellow.

" I reached for my copies of *Hegel* and *Locke*,
    Longinus and *Plato*, although
Sun shone on the rectory tennis court,
    I am agnostic, you know.

" Jolly old Winchester ! jolly old New College !
    Cream of our fine middle classes !
By cheerful unbendings in soccer and social clubs,
    We can get on with the masses."

THE WYKEHAMIST

(To Randolph Churchill, but not about him.)

 R O A D of Church and " broad of mind,"
Broad before and broad behind,
A keen ecclesiologist,
A rather dirty Wykehamist.
'Tis not for us to wonder why
He wears that curious knitted tie ;
We should not cast reflections on
The very slightest kind of don.
We should not giggle as we like
At his appearance on his bike ;
It's something to become a bore,
And more than that, at twenty-four.
It's something too to know your wants
And go full pelt for Norman fonts.
Just now the chestnut trees are dark
And full with shadow in the park,
And " six o'clock " St. Mary calls
Above the mellow college walls.
The evening stretches arms to twist
And captivate her Wykehamist.
But not for him those autumn days,
He shuts them out with heavy baize ;
He gives his Ovaltine a stir
And nibbles at a " petit beurre ",
And, satisfying fleshy wants,
He settles down to Norman fonts.

DEATH IN LEAMINGTON

HE died in the upstairs bedroom
  By the light of the ev'ning star
That shone through the plate glass window
  From over Leamington Spa.

Beside her the lonely crochet
  Lay patiently and unstirred,
But the fingers that would have work'd it
  Were dead as the spoken word.

And Nurse came in with the tea-things
  Breast high 'mid the stands and chairs—
But Nurse was alone with her own little soul,
  And the things were alone with theirs.

She bolted the big round window,
  She let the blinds unroll,
She set a match to the mantel,
  She covered the fire with coal.

And " Tea ! " she said in a tiny voice
  " Wake up !   It's nearly *five*."
Oh ! Chintzy, chintzy cheeriness,
  Half dead and half alive !

Do you know that the stucco is peeling ?
  Do you know that the heart will stop ?
From those yellow Italianate arches
  Do you hear the plaster drop ?

24

Nurse looked at the silent bedstead,
    At the gray, decaying face,
As the calm of a Leamington ev'ning
    Drifted into the place.

She moved the table of bottles
    Away from the bed to the wall,
And tiptoeing gently over the stairs
    Turned down the gas in the hall.

26

HYMN

HE Church's Restoration
In eighteen-eighty-three
Has left for contemplation
Not what there used to be.
How well the ancient woodwork
Looks round the Rect'ry hall,
Memorial of the good work
Of him who plann'd it all,

He who took down the pew-ends
And sold them anywhere
But kindly spared a few ends
Work'd up into a chair.
O worthy persecution
Of dust !   O hue divine !
O cheerful substitution,
Thou varnishéd pitch-pine !

Church furnishing !   Church furnishing !
Sing art and crafty praise !
He gave the brass for burnishing,
He gave the thick red baize,
He gave the new addition,
Pull'd down the dull old aisle,
—To pave the sweet transition
He gave th' encaustic tile.

Of marble brown and veinéd
   He did the pulpit make ;
He order'd windows stainéd
   Light red and crimson lake.
Sing on, with hymns uproarious,
   Ye humble and aloof,
Look up ! and oh how glorious
   He has restored the roof !

AN EIGHTEENTH-CENTURY CALVINISTIC HYMN

HANK God my Afflictions are such
That I cannot lie down on my Bed,
And if I but take to my Couch
I incessantly Vomit and Bleed.

I am not too sure of my Worth,
Indeed it is tall as a Palm;
But what Fruits can it ever bring forth
When Leprosy sits at the Helm?

Though Torment's the Soul's Goal's Rewards
The contrary's Proof of my Guilt,
While Dancing, Backgammon and Cards
Are among the worst Symptoms I've felt.

Oh! I bless the good Lord for my Boils,
For my mental and bodily pains,
For without them my Faith all congeals
And I'm doomed to HELL'S NE'ER-ENDING FLAMES.

THIS cold weather
Carries so many old people away.
Quavering voices and blankets and breath
Go silent together.
The gentle fingers are touching to pray
Which crumple and straighten for Death.
These cold breezes
Carry the bells away on the air,

Stuttering tales
of Gothic, and
pass,
Catching new
grave flowers
into their hair
Beating the
chapel and
red-coloured
glass.

THE SANDEMANIAN MEETING-HOUSE IN
HIGHBURY QUADRANT

N roaring iron down the Holloway Road
The red trams and the brown trams pour,
And little each yellow-faced jolted load
Knows of the fast-shut grained oak door.

From Canonbury, Dalston and Mildmay Park
The old North London shoots in a train
To the long black platform, gaslit and dark,
Oh Highbury Station once and again.

Steam or electric, little they care,
Yellow brick terrace or terra-cotta hall,
White-wood sweet shop or silent square,
That the LORD OF THE SCRIPTURES is LORD OF ALL.

Away from the barks and the shouts and the greetings,
Psalm-singing over and love-lunch done,
Listening to the Bible in their room for meetings,
Old Sandemanians are hidden from the sun.

COMPETITION

HE Independent Calvinistic   1810
    Methodist Chapel is gone,
    Dust in the galleries, dust on the stairs,
    There was no one to carry it on.
And a Norman New Jerusalem Church   1840
  Was raised on the sacred site,
Where they praised the Lord and praised the Lord
  By incandescent light.

The Gothic is bursting over the way
  With Evangelical Song,
For the pinnacled Wesley Memorial Church   1860
  Is over a hundred strong,
And what is a new Jerusalem
  Gas-lit and yellow wall'd
To a semi-circular pitchpine sea
  With electric light install'd ?

Crack your walls, Wesley Memorial !
  Shine bright, you electrolier !
Your traceried windows may rock with song,
  New Jerusalem fall in fear ;
Short lived ! Short lived ! in this world of ours
  Are Triumph and Praise and Prayer !
What of Mount Carmel Baptists (Strict),   1875
  For they've central heating there ?

33

34

TUNBRIDGE WELLS

UNBRIDGE WELLS on a Lord's Day Morning,
Rung from rest by the Gospel Bells,
Climbs to light through the mist adorning
Towers and steeples of Tunbridge Wells.

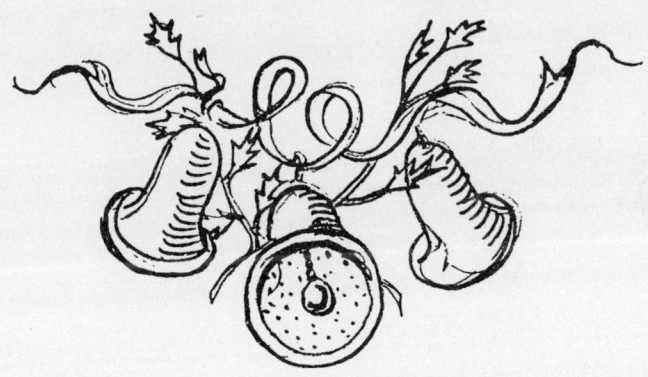

CAMBERLEY

WONDER whether you would make
A friend of Mrs. Kittiwake ?
Colonel Kittiwake, it's true,
Is not the sort of man for you.
I'll tell you how to get to know
Their cosy little bungalow.
When sunset gilds the Surrey pines
The fam'ly usually dines.
So later, in the Surrey dark,
Make for Poonah Punkah Park,
And by the monument to Clive
You'll come to Enniscorthy Drive,
Coolgreena is the last of all,
And mind the terrier when you call.

The drawing-room is done in pink,
The other rooms are mauve, I think.
So when you see electric light
Behind pink curtains it's all right.
Knock gently, don't disturb the maid,
She's got to clear, and I'm afraid
That she is less inclined to take
The blame than Mrs. Kittiwake.

THE OUTER SUBURBS

THE weary walk from Oakley Park
Through the soft suburban dark
Bedizened with electric lights
Which stream across these Northern Heights.
In blackened blocks against the view
Stands gabled Rosslyn Avenue,
And bright within each kitchenette
The things for morning tea are set.
A stained glass window, red and green,
Shines, hiding what should not be seen,
While wifie knits through hubbie's gloom
Safe in the Drage-way drawing-room,
Oh how expectant for the bed
All " Jacobethan " overhead !

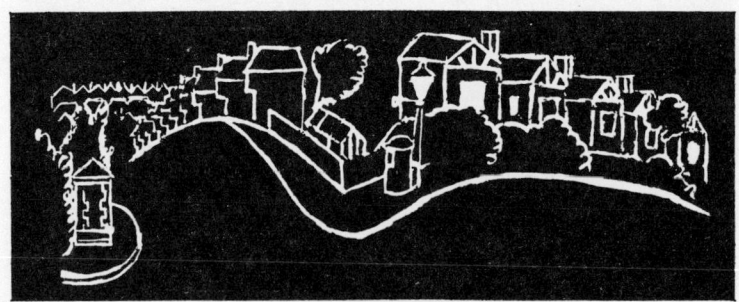

THE FLIGHT FROM BOOTLE

ONELY in the Regent Palace,
Sipping her " Banana Blush ",
Lilian lost sight of Alice
In the honey-coloured rush.

Settled down at last from Bootle,
Alice whispered, " Just a min,
While I pop upstairs and rootle
For another safety pin ".

Dreamy from the band pavilion
Drops of the *Immortal Hour*
Fell around the lonely Lilian
Like an ineffectual shower.

Half an hour she sat and waited
In the honey-coloured lounge,
Till she with herself debated,
" Time for me to go and scrounge ! "

Time enough ! or not enough time !
Lilian, you wait in vain ;
Alice will not have a rough time,
Nor be quite the same again.

40

CROYDON

N a house like that
Your Uncle Dick was born ;
Satchel on back he walked to Whitgift
Every weekday morn.

Boys together in Coulsdon woodlands,
  Bramble-berried and steep,
He and his pals would look for spadgers
  Hidden deep.

The laurels are speckled in Marchmont Avenue
  Just as they were before,
But the steps are dirty that still lead up to
  Your Uncle Dick's front door.

Pear and apple in Croydon gardens
  Bud and blossom fall,
But your Uncle Dick has left his Croydon
  Once for all.

THE GARDEN CITY

 WOT ye why in Orchard Way
The roofs be steep and shelving ?
Or wot ye what the dwellers say
In close and garden delving ?

" Belike unlike my hearths to yours,
 Yet seemly if unlike them.
Deep green and stalwart be my doors
 With bottle glass to fryke* them.

" Hand-woven be my wefts, hand-made
 My pottery for pottage,
And hoe and mattock, aye, and spade,
 Hang up about my cottage."

Men of Welwyn ! Men of Worth !
 The Health Reform is growing,
With Parsley girdled round the earth
 That recks not of its sowing.

* Mediæval word for " deck."

43

WESTGATE-ON-SEA

ARK, I hear the bells of Westgate,
   I will tell you what they sigh,
Where those minarets and steeples
   Prick the open Thanet sky.

Happy bells of eighteen-ninety,
   Bursting from your freestone tower !
Recalling laurel, shrubs and privet,
   Red geraniums in flower,

Feet that scamper on the asphalt,
   Through the Borough Council grass,
Till they hide inside the shelter
   Bright with ironwork and glass,

Striving chains of ordered children
   Purple by the sea-breeze made,
Striving on to prunes and suet
   Past the shops on the Parade,

Some with wire around their glasses,
   Some with wire across their teeth,
Writhing frames for running noses
   And the drooping lip beneath.

Church of England bells of Westgate !
   On this balcony I stand,
White the woodwork wriggles round me,
   Clock towers rise on either hand.

For me in my timber arbour
   You have one more message yet,
" Plimsolls, plimsolls in the summer,
   Oh goloshes in the wet ! "

" New King arrives in his
capital by air. . ."
                    Daily Newspaper.

PIRITS of well-shot woodcock, partridge, snipe
Flutter and bear him up the Norfolk sky :
In that red house in a red mahogany book-case
The stamp collection waits with mounts long dry.
The big blue eyes are shut which saw wrong clothing
And favourite fields and coverts from a horse ;
Old men in country houses hear clocks ticking
Over thick carpets with a deadened force ;
Old men who never cheated, never doubted,
Communicated monthly, sit and stare
At a red suburb ruled by Lady Liner
Where a young man lands hatless from the air.